The Five Guiding Principles

Principles

A Resource for Study

The Five Guiding Principles

A Resource for Study

**The Faith and Order Commission
of the Church of England**

CHURCH HOUSE
PUBLISHING

Church House Publishing
Church House
Great Smith Street
London SW1P 3AZ

ISBN 978 0 7151 1135 2

       978 0 7151 1136 9   Core Source

       978 0 7151 1137 6   Kindle

Published 2018 for the Faith and Order Commission
of the Church of England by Church House Publishing

Typeset by ForDesign

Printed in the UK by

Contents

Foreword

The Faith and Order Commission has been aware for some time of requests for theological commentary on the Five Guiding Principles set out in the *House of Bishops' Declaration on the Ministry of Bishops and Priests* in 2014. They have come from people engaged in explaining to other churches the distinctive approach the Church of England has taken on the ordination of women to the episcopate, including the provision made for those who do not accept the ministry of female clergy. They have also come from staff at Theological Education Institutions responsible for teaching ordinands about the Five Guiding Principles, who would like to be able to point them to appropriate resources.

When the *Review of Nomination to the See of Sheffield and Related Concerns* was published as a report from the Independent Reviewer in September 2017, some progress had already been made by the Commission in beginning to draft a resource that could meet these needs. At paragraph 198, the Independent Reviewer recommended:

> that the House invites the Faith and Order Commission to examine the theological challenge which has been posed to the 2014 Settlement and that the results of this work, together with the House's response to the pastoral challenge I have identified in paragraph 192, inform the ongoing process of discussion and education about the Settlement for which I have also called.

While the work that was already in hand did not seek to address directly the controversy associated with the subject of the Independent Reviewer's report, the Commission hopes its publication can contribute significantly to 'the ongoing process of discussion and education about the Settlement', the importance of which has now come sharply into focus. As a resource for study, it aims to support thinking and dialogue about some of the significant issues that have arisen in light of 'the theological challenge which has been posed to the 2014 Settlement'.

After a brief introduction that clarifies the character and purpose of the Five Guiding Principles, the first main chapter of the document that follows briefly sketches the events over the last three decades from which they emerged. The second and most substantial chapter offers a commentary on each of the Five Guiding Principles in turn, highlighting key aspects and analysing some of the theological issues that they raise. The third chapter then looks as what it means to live out the Five Guiding Principles in the context of the life of the Church of England. A short final chapter offers questions for further reflection, which could be drawn on for group discussion and dialogue as well as for consideration by individual readers.

We hope this resource will be useful for understanding the thinking that lies behind the Five Guiding Principles, and the context in which they originated. We also hope that it may encourage all those who read it to think carefully about what it means to be guided by these principles in 'making every effort to maintain the unity of the Spirit in the bond of peace' (Ephesians 4.3).

The Rt Revd Dr Christopher Cocksworth
Chair of the Faith and Order Commission

Introduction

The Five Guiding Principles

i. Now that legislation has been passed to enable women to become bishops the Church of England is fully and unequivocally committed to all orders of ministry being open equally to all, without reference to gender, and holds that those whom it has duly ordained and appointed to office are the true and lawful holders of the office which they occupy and thus deserve due respect and canonical obedience;

ii. Anyone who ministers within the Church of England must be prepared to acknowledge that the Church of England has reached a clear decision on the matter;

iii. Since it continues to share the historic episcopate with other Churches, including the Roman Catholic Church, the Orthodox Church and those provinces of the Anglican Communion which continue to ordain only men as priests or bishops, the Church of England acknowledges that its own clear decision on ministry and gender is set within a broader process of discernment within the Anglican Communion and the whole Church of God;

iv. Since those within the Church of England who, on grounds of theological conviction, are unable to receive the ministry of women bishops or priests continue to be within the spectrum of teaching and tradition of the Anglican Communion, the Church of England remains committed to enabling them to flourish within its life and structures; and

v. Pastoral and sacramental provision for the minority within the Church of England will be made without specifying a limit of time and in a way that maintains the highest possible degree of communion and contributes to mutual flourishing across the whole Church of England.[1]

When the Archbishop of Canterbury appeared, with others, before the Ecclesiastical Committee of Parliament following the General Synod's Final Approval of the Measure to approve the admission of women to the episcopate, he was asked about the Five Guiding Principles and the theology which undergirds them. He replied that the Five Guiding Principles constitute 'a promise to seek to love one another', and said that they are 'not a deal.' He went on, likewise, to suggest that the way to put them into practice was to 'love one another. Wash each other's feet. Love your neighbour. Love your enemy.'[2] Introducing the Five Guiding Principles at the General Synod in February 2014, the Archbishop had similarly said that 'they are short and to the point and they depend on love and trust.'[3]

It is right to begin this short text on the Five Guiding Principles with these references, by the Archbishop of Canterbury, to the gift and virtue of love – *caritas*.[4] To do so is to recognize that, in any context, the living out of principles is dependent on the fostering of associated virtues, and that in the particular context of the life of the church, our most strenuous efforts to do what duty and devotion appear to require are worth nothing at all without love (1 Corinthians 13.1–3).

The Five Guiding Principles arose from a situation of deep and serious disagreement within the Church of England about the theology and practice of church order, with a strong desire nonetheless to keep open space within the one Church of England for different views on this matter to be held. They formed one (crucial) part of a package of measures introduced in 2014, when the Church of England agreed to admit women to the episcopate and thereby open its three orders of ministry –

deacons, priests, and bishops – to all, without reference to gender. Not everyone welcomed this change, and so the Five Guiding Principles provide some basic parameters to help Anglicans with different theological convictions on this matter continue to relate to each other within one church.

The imperative of love, however, means that such accommodation of difference can never simply be about the right to hold a private opinion, or the toleration of a minority view. Love seeks the good of the other – and one way to express the good for people is in terms of their flourishing.[5] Hence, as the Archbishop of Canterbury expressed it: 'I say again that the Church of England is deeply committed to the flourishing of all those who are part of its life in the grace of God. It is not our intention that any particular group should wither on the vine.'[6]

The Five Guiding Principles are therefore intended to be life-giving; they are about opening up the space in which Christians of differing theological convictions and different practices on a critical question of church order can be true disciples of Jesus Christ within the one Church of England. This is the main hermeneutic by which to unlock the point and practice of the Five Guiding Principles. They are not about defining the minimum which is required for fulfilment of the law, but rather an invitation to all to act with maximum grace – with sharp challenges thereby being posed for everyone involved, some of them varying according to the positions people hold. In July 2014, on the occasion of the final vote on the *Bishops and Priests (Consecration and Ordination of Women)* Measure, the Archbishop underlined that living out the Five Guiding Principles 'will be hard work. Progress will be all but impossible to achieve without a fresh embrace of one another in the love that Jesus Christ gives us by his Spirit.'[7]

The Five Guiding Principles are not, then, merely a 'deal' that allows a truce between campaigners. Nor are they a set of rules that must be observed if sanctions are to be avoided. Nor are they a piece of concise systematic theology outlining the approach the Church of England has taken. They are instead, as suggested by the Archbishop of Canterbury, a 'promise' and a pledge for all in the Church of England to take up,[8] in the knowledge that to do so is to respond to an invitation which comes with some serious challenges for all. The promise will only be kept, the invitation only accepted and the challenges only met as we are obedient to Paul's command to 'clothe yourselves with love, which binds everything together in perfect harmony' (Colossians 3.14). That love is the gift of the Holy Spirit, the gift that makes and transforms the Church.

Chapter 1   How Did We Get Here?

The Five Guiding Principles were drafted in the aftermath of the defeat
at the November group of sessions of the Church of England's General
Synod in 2012 of draft legislation to enable women to be made bishops.
There had been widespread shock on the part of many involved when
this happened, and perplexity too about what would happen next. This
first chapter briefly sets out the story of how the Five Guiding Principles
came to be written, and to play a crucial role in the approval of new
legislation in 2014.

Towards the ordination of women to the priesthood

The General Synod of the Church of England gave Final Approval to
a Measure to allow women to be ordained as priests on the 11th
November 1992, and the first women were so ordained on the 12th
March 1994.[9] These events were themselves the conclusion of years
of debate and discussion within the church; the first Church of England
report to comment on the question of ordaining women was published
just after the end of the First World War, in 1919.[10] Similar debates have
been held in many other churches; some have decided to change their
polity so as to enable the ordination of women to all orders of ministry.
In the Roman Catholic Church, the tradition of restricting the ordained
ministry to men has been upheld by recent papal teaching. One
distinguishing feature of the dialogue within the Church of England,
however, was a concern only to proceed with the ordination of women as
priests if there was appropriate provision for those who could not accept
their ministry as priests to remain fully a part of the Church of England.

The draft Measure that emerged in July 1988 proposed that women might be ordained to the office of priest, while explicitly excluding the admission of women to the episcopate. The safeguards for opponents included the basis of what would become Resolutions 'A' and 'B' in the successful Measure (these effectively prevented a female priest from presiding at Holy Communion or pronouncing the absolution in a parish, or being appointed as its incumbent or priest-in-charge), together with a provision, never in fact exercised, that a diocesan bishop could declare that women could not be ordained or authorised to minister as priests in his diocese. During the debate on the draft Measure in 1989, there was an attempt to limit the safeguards to 20 years: it was decisively lost. Eventually, on 11 November 1992, General Synod gave final approval to the Priests (Ordination of Women) Measure.

The Act of Synod

In the wake of the vote in November 1992, however, the House of Bishops decided that further provisions would be required to deal with the consequences of the impaired communion which would now extend to the relationship between bishops who ordained women to the priesthood and those clergy and laity who could not receive the sacramental ministry of female priests. These provisions, informed by extensive discussion on the part of Parliament's Ecclesiastical Committee, formed the basis of the Episcopal Ministry Act of Synod. It was approved by all three Houses of the General Synod in November 1993 and promulged in 1994.[11] The thinking which informed the provisions of the Act had been sketched out in the June 1993 report of the House of Bishops, *Bonds of Peace*, which itself drew from an accompanying paper on the ecclesiological issues at stake, *Being in Communion.*[12]

The Act of Synod has an important place within this story, because its terms and provisions provide a crucial part of the background for the Five Guiding Principles. The Preamble to the Act stated that it was passed in order 'to make provision for the continuing diversity of opinion in the Church of England as to the ordination and ministry of women as priests.' The Act confirmed that the bishop of each diocese continued as the Ordinary of his diocese – a fundamental building-block of Anglican polity which has persisted, and which is reasserted in the first Guiding Principle. The Act then offered three propositions, which find parallels in the third, fourth and fifth Guiding Principles in particular:

(3) The General Synod regards it as desirable that –

    (a) all concerned should endeavour to ensure that –

        (i) discernment in the wider Church of the rightness or otherwise of the Church of England's decision to ordain women to the priesthood should be as open a process as possible;

        (ii) the highest possible degree of communion should be maintained within each diocese; and

        (iii) the integrity of differing beliefs and positions concerning the ordination of women to the priesthood should be mutually recognised and respected.

From 1994 to 2012

In the Church of England, six years after the first women had been ordained to the priesthood, the General Synod passed a motion calling for theological study of the issues posed by ordaining women as bishops. This resulted in 2004 in the publication of a substantial report, *Women Bishops in the Church of England?*, which thoroughly examined the key issues and provided the foundation for all further work in this area.[13] The year after that, the General Synod resolved to set in train the process which would lead to legislation enabling the admission of women to the episcopate. In 2006, it passed a motion affirming that the ordination of women as bishops would be consonant with the faith of the Church as the Church of England had received it, and would be a proper development.

In July 2008, the General Synod debated the general shape which the legislation for this should take. The draft Measure came back to Synod for Final Approval in November 2012 but failed to achieve the required majority in the House of Laity. A significant factor for some members of the House of Laity, themselves personally convinced of the rightness of ordaining women to the episcopate, was their belief that the draft Measure did not contain adequate provision for those who were unable to accept in an unqualified manner the ministry of women as bishops.

The path to female bishops 2012–14

In the aftermath of these events, there was a firm resolve to find a fresh way forward, on the part both of those in favour of, and those opposed to, the ordination of women to the episcopate. A new working group was established, calling for new arrangements based on 'simplicity; reciprocity; and mutuality', and it made remarkably swift progress given the time it had taken for the previous proposals to be assembled. Key to this was the articulation of the Five Guiding Principles, first formulated for the May meeting of the House of Bishops in 2013 by the working group, and then included in the report from the House of Bishops for the General Synod in July of the same year.[14]

A consensus began to emerge around legislation that was much simpler and would not replicate the lengthy Code of Practice accompanying the failed Measure. A very short Measure opening the episcopate to women, accompanied by a House of Bishops' Declaration, of which the Five Guiding Principles formed a part, and a new Canon enshrining a disputes resolution procedure, made it to final approval within twelve months. General Synod welcomed the Five Guiding Principles, commended by the House of Bishops in May 2013, in its resolution of 20 November 2013. The draft Measure was given Final Approval in July 2014, and the new canon promulged in November 2014. The first female bishop, the Revd Libby Lane, was consecrated Bishop of Stockport in January 2015. The next month, the Revd Philip North, a traditional Anglo-Catholic, was consecrated Bishop of Burnley. A new era in the life of the Church of England had begun.

Chapter 2 The Five Guiding Principles in Focus

The Five Guiding Principles lie at the heart of the House of Bishops' *Declaration on the Ministry of Bishops and Priests* (May 2014).[15] They are expected to be affirmed by every candidate for ordination in the Church of England, before and during their ordination training.[16]

Clergy and candidates for ordained ministry might find some of the Guiding Principles more appealing than others, but the *Declaration* insists that all five 'need to be read one with the other and held together in tension, rather than being applied selectively'. In this chapter, each of the Guiding Principles is examined in turn, with careful attention to what it means for them to 'be read one with the other and held together in tension'.

Guiding Principle No. 1

- **Now that legislation has been passed to enable women to become bishops the Church of England is fully and unequivocally committed to all orders of ministry being open equally to all, without reference to gender, and holds that those whom it has duly ordained and appointed to office are the true and lawful holders of the office which they occupy and thus deserve due respect and canonical obedience.**

The first Guiding Principle states two things: the commitment of the Church of England that all orders of ministry are to be 'open equally to all', and its declared position that, alongside other clergy, all bishops 'duly ordained and appointed to office' are 'true and lawful holders of the office'. There is no equivocation on this point, as if the Church of England considered this something that remains to any extent uncertain.

The first Guiding Principle refers both to 'orders of ministry' and 'office'. According to the doctrine of the Church of England, there are three orders of ministry – deacon, priest and bishop – and ordination to those orders confers a 'character' of which the person can never be 'divested' (Canon C 1.1–2). An 'office' in this context means the appointment that a particular ordained person may hold, which could be a see in the case of a bishop or e.g. an incumbency in the case of a priest. All those who are ordained to the episcopate and hold episcopal office in the church 'deserve due respect and canonical obedience.' Such respect is not to be accorded out of kindness or goodwill only: it is deserved, not because of the merits of the office holder, but because of the position that the Church of England maintains as to what it is doing when it ordains people and appoints them to offices. Furthermore, priests and deacons owe 'canonical obedience' to their diocesan bishop 'in all things lawful and honest' (Canon C 1.3). At threshold moments in their ministry, such as ordination and licensing, that obedience is vocalized in the form of an oath (Canon C 14). This does not mean a blanket agreement to follow every episcopal instruction, but to obey those instructions which the bishop is authorized to give under canon law.[17] The gender of the diocesan bishop is no grounds for refusing the oath or for limiting its scope. The House of Bishops has said it believes that all ministers of the Church of England will be able, in good conscience, to take the oath.[18]

This was summed up by the Archbishop of Canterbury, in answer to a question from a member of the Ecclesiastical Committee about the Five Guiding Principles, when he said that they embody first 'a very simple statement that women will be bishops.'[19] The first Guiding Principle enshrines, in short, the clear will of the majority of the General Synod (and the overwhelming majority of the Diocesan Synods) that the office of bishop should be open to women as well as to men, and that the Church of England should, in every respect, speak only of bishops (and priests and deacons) and not of 'women bishops' (or 'women priests' and 'women deacons').

The final clause in the first Guiding Principle makes clear that the advent of bishops who are women does not alter the legal and canonical structures of the Church of England. A female bishop who is appointed to a diocesan See becomes, on confirmation of election, the Ordinary[20] of that diocese with all the rights and responsibilities belonging to that office. As Archbishop Rowan Williams said to General Synod in February 2012:

> We want clarity, it seems, about a single structure for the diocesan episcopate. We have not been sympathetic to any idea of parallel or quasi-independent jurisdictions. We want to see, as has often been said, bishops being bishops rather than different kinds of bishops with different kinds of powers.[21]

The first Guiding Principle raises the challenge of recognition. What does it mean for someone who is not convinced that women can exercise episcopal ministry to give 'due respect and canonical obedience' to a bishop who is a woman? While it would be possible to focus here on the minimum that is required for conformity with ecclesiastical law, to do so risks divorcing the office itself from the person holding that office, in a way that undermines both ecclesiology and personal relationships.

The language sometimes used in this context is of 'recognizing' other people's orders, or 'recognizing me as a priest'. A straightforward and overt contradiction between how I see myself and how you see me in any human relationship is hard to navigate, and potentially a source of great pain. There is however no simple way to close the gap here so that the tension vanishes.

Ordained ministry is ecclesial and public as well as personal, and therefore to question the confidence with which a priest or bishop's ministry can be received is not only to register a certain reservation about the self-identity of the ordained person but also about the life of the church communities that receive their ministry. It needs to be remembered that there are a variety of Anglican theologies of ordained ministry, and therefore a different weight placed on the idea of 'recognition of orders' by, for example, Evangelicals and Catholics. Yet careful consideration of what we do 'recognize' in one another within the body of Christ, and of the best theological description that can be offered for that, is needed if 'respect' is to be fully expressed and communicated as a characteristic of our relationships.

The first Guiding Principle also points to the ecclesial significance of belonging to the same church polity, with the same Canon Law. Although not every member of the Church of England may, in conscience, feel able to receive the sacrament at every celebration of the Eucharist (because not every member may receive the sacramental ministry of every president or celebrant), this impairment of communion does not amount to wholesale separation. The Church of England remains united in one canonical structure; its 'councils' remain common to all and their decisions equally binding on upon all. This form of conciliarity is not only about legal and structural arrangements but about the kind of relationships that they enable within the life of the body of Christ here on earth.[22]

Guiding Principle No. 2

- **Anyone who ministers within the Church of England must be prepared to acknowledge that the Church of England has reached a clear decision on the matter.**

The second Guiding Principle builds upon the first. Ministers in the Church of England, regardless of their own theological views, can be in no doubt that the Church corporately has made a clear decision. Although churches and synods can and do err (Articles XIX and XXI of the Thirty-Nine Articles), the Church of England has no intention to re-open this question. If ministers are to contribute constructively to the wider life of the Church of England they must acknowledge this state of affairs, which is not to say that they must support the decision that was taken.

The Church of England's decision to welcome women as bishops – and thus to open all three orders of ministry to women and men equally – was reached after many decades of study, debate and prayer. It was not a decision taken lightly or rashly. The proposals that eventually enabled women to be ordained as bishops in the Church of England, which included provision for those who would not be able to receive their ministry and for which the Five Guiding Principles themselves were key, received overwhelming support in the councils of the church. Forty-three diocesan synods considered the question, and all voted in favour. In total 3799 votes were cast in these diocesan synods, with 114 abstentions. Counting abstentions, 88% voted in favour. Not counting abstentions, 91% voted in favour – 96% of bishops, 90% of clergy, and 92% of laity.[23]

In the General Synod, the agreement was also substantial: House of Bishops 95% (37 in favour, 2 against, 1 abstention), House of Clergy 87% (162 in favour, 25 against, 4 abstentions), House of Laity 77% (152 in favour, 45 against, 5 abstentions).[24] There remains, of course, a significant minority in the Church of England which regrets this change of policy, and some voted in favour of the proposals who did not support the ordination of women as bishops but believed the proposal were the best way forward for the Church of England in the circumstances. The Church of England's corporate decision, as represented by its synods, is however clear.

Guiding Principle No. 3

- Since it continues to share the historic episcopate with other Churches, including the Roman Catholic Church, the Orthodox Church and those provinces of the Anglican Communion which continue to ordain only men as priests or bishops, the Church of England acknowledges that its own clear decision on ministry and gender is set within a

broader process of discernment within the Anglican Communion and the whole Church of God.

The third Guiding Principle widens the horizons for understanding what the Church of England has done, to a global and inter-denominational context. The Church of England does not own the 'historic episcopate', but receives it as part of the ancient common tradition and shares it with other churches; to use a phrase of Rowan Williams, it aspires to offer and participate in 'a ministry capable of universal acceptance.'[25] Therefore any significant change in the way that *episcope* finds expression within the Church of England must be in dialogue with those churches with whom it shares the historic episcopate, including the Roman Catholic Church, the Orthodox Churches, some Lutheran churches and other provinces of the Anglican Communion.

The dialogue within the Anglican Communion regarding the ordination of women is reflected in significant resolutions of the Lambeth Conference. In 1988, for instance, the bishops of the Communion agreed in the first Resolution of the Conference:

1.   That each province respect the decision and attitudes of other provinces in the ordination or consecration of women to the episcopate, without such respect necessarily indicating acceptance of the principles involved, maintaining the highest possible degree of communion with the provinces which differ.

2. That bishops exercise courtesy and maintain communications with bishops who may differ, and with any woman bishop, ensuring an open dialogue in the Church to whatever extent communion is impaired.[26]

Ten years later, in 1998, they called upon the churches of the Anglican Communion to 'uphold the principle of "open Reception" as it relates to the ordination of women to the priesthood... noting that "reception is a long and spiritual process"' (Resolution III.2).[27]

The importance of attention to the views of the wider church was already highlighted in a passage from *Bonds of Peace* that speaks of 'the ongoing process of the discernment of truth within the wider fellowship of the Christian Church.'[28] Elsewhere, the same report stressed that 'Discernment of the matter is now to be seen within a much broader and larger process of discernment within the whole Church under the Spirit's guidance.'[29] Consultation between the Church of England and the Roman Catholic Church in the period leading up to the decisive debates of 2014 included a lengthy response from the Catholic Bishops' Conference of England and Wales to an invitation to ecumenical partners for comment, and Cardinal Walter Kasper's address to the House of Bishops in 2006.[30] That is not to underestimate, however, the difficulty for the relationship between the Church of England and the Roman Catholic Church as a result of increased divergence on this matter.

This third Guiding Principle stands in a particularly close relationship to its predecessor, which stresses that the Church of England has made a clear decision, one which it believes to be according to the will of God and consonant with the witness of the scriptures. The Church of England does not claim to be able to make decisions for the universal church, but considers this broadening of the episcopate to be consistent with its position as 'part of the One, Holy, Catholic and Apostolic Church' (Preface to the Declaration of Assent, as set out in Canon C 15).

The Church of England is committed to striving for the full visible unity of Christ's church, and therefore to seeking the will of Christ *with* the whole church.[31] As the ARCIC document *Authority in the Church* (1976) noted: 'Shared commitment and belief create a common mind in determining how the gospel should be interpreted and obeyed.'[32] The third Guiding Principle speaks of 'a broader process of discernment' which extends to 'the whole church of God', emphasizing that this process goes beyond the churches that share the 'historic episcopate' to include non-episcopal churches, which have themselves come to different conclusions regarding women and ordained ministry. For some, such as the Methodist Church, the Church of England's acceptance of women as bishops has removed a potential obstacle to deeper communion. This will not, however, be the case for all.

Discernment in this context overlaps to some extent with the important concept in recent ecclesiology of 'reception', referred to in Resolution III.2 of the 1998 Lambeth Conference as cited above (page 25). This idea was developed in the latter part of the twentieth century from its origins in canon law, by Roman Catholic scholars in particular, and was then widely taken up by the ecumenical movement; it is developed in significant ways in dialogues between the Anglican Communion and other global communions.[33] The focus in the third Guiding Principle, however, is specifically on discernment as a task that cannot be undertaken by the Church of England in isolation, but which it addresses as a church within the Anglican Communion and as a part of the whole Church of God. Its having come to 'a clear decision on the matter' does not mean that it has no interest or part in the 'wider process of discernment' that is continuing.

Guiding Principle No. 4

- **Since those within the Church of England who, on grounds of theological conviction, are unable to receive the ministry of women bishops or priests continue to be within the spectrum of teaching and tradition of the Anglican Communion, the Church of England remains committed to enabling them to flourish within its life and structures.**

The fourth Guiding Principle appears to stand in some tension with the first. Indeed, when introducing the Five Guiding Principles in General Synod, the Bishop of Rochester spoke of 'the deliberate but hopefully creative tension between the first and the fourth bullet'.[34] Is it really a creative tension, however, or a straightforward contradiction? How can the Church of England be 'fully and unequivocally committed to all orders of ministry being open equally to all, without reference to gender' and, at the same time, enable the 'flourishing' of those who 'on grounds of theological conviction, are unable to receive the ministry of women bishops or priests'? In order to address this conundrum, there are some key words and phrases that need further attention.

The first is 'theological conviction'.[35] It is not legitimate to decline to receive the ministry of female bishops and priests simply because of personal preference, local custom, or any kind of prejudice. But this Guiding Principle acknowledges that there are genuinely 'theological' reasons why some might not receive this ministry, perhaps on grounds of scriptural exegesis or understanding of catholic order.

The concept of theological conviction is closely related to the concept of integrity. The Act of Synod in 1993 stated that 'the integrity of differing beliefs and positions concerning the ordination of women to the priesthood should be mutually recognised and respected.'[36] Such respect for the integrity of one another's theological convictions means that those opposed to the ordination of women should not characterize those in favour as caving in to the fashions of the age, and nor should those in favour stigmatise those opposed as supporters of discrimination and injustice. Such attitudes render the operation of the Five Guiding Principles unworkable. Of course, flawed motivations may coexist with properly theological reasons, but one cannot deny the existence of the latter because the former may also be in play. Nor should we imagine that because we have good theological reasons for our own position, we are therefore wholly innocent of sinful desires in the actions we take to further it.

This approach needs to be carefully distinguished from the misuse of the language of the Act of Synod as if there are two ecclesiological 'integrities' within the Church of England.[37] The fourth Guiding Principle asserts that those who dissent for theological reasons from the 'clear decision' of the Church of England on this matter are not simply to be tolerated on the margins of the church, or respectfully accommodated within parallel structures that keep them at arm's length, but are to be enabled to 'flourish in its life and structures'. To 'flourish' has connotations of to prosper, to thrive, to grow – not to shrink out and die. It means prayerfully encouraging all within the Church of England, that they might prove fruitful in proclaiming the kingdom of God, not wanting any to dwindle or fail. It means not corralling some within the boundaries of their own parishes or networks, but providing space generously for all to flourish in its common life and in structures shared by all. 'Equal treatment, for example in relation to resource issues and the discerning of vocations to the ordained ministry, is essential irrespective of convictions in relation to gender and ministry.'[38] It is here that the Five Guiding Principles most clearly move beyond anything that had been said overtly in previous Anglican documents and statements on this issue.

But how can we support the flourishing of those whose views we think are not only mistaken but harmful, and indeed harmful for the life of the church? This is an important question, and one with which people who take up different positions on this question may need to struggle. If I cannot be sure, for instance, that women may be priests and bishops, then it is at least possible that those who receive their ministry suffer in various ways in consequence, while prospects for unity with Catholic and Orthodox churches, who make up the majority of the world's Christians, are being damaged beyond easily imaginable repair. If I believe that God calls women and men to be priests, then it is at least possible that those who teach otherwise are helping to prevent women with a vocation to ordained ministry from fulfilling their calling before God, obstructing the church as a whole from receiving the fullness of the gifts Christ would give it and impeding its witness to a world that desperately needs to hear the good news of abundant life.

One answer to this question would be to say that the flourishing we seek for one another in the church is ultimately defined by the goal of growing up 'to maturity, to the measure of the full stature of Christ' (Ephesians 4.13). For all of us, such flourishing is likely to mean change and challenge, repentance and deepening conversion. It certainly does not mean being left alone to continue as we are. Part of what it means to seek the flourishing of those with whom we disagree – and who may even espouse views we regard as harmful – specifically as something that can unfold within 'the life and structures' of the one Church of England is that we will take no action intended to exclude them, marginalise them or jeopardise their place alongside us, because it is within this one church and together with us that we hope and pray for them to grow up to maturity. That is about exercising a certain practical discipline of restraint, alongside persuasion and constant prayer for our maturity together according to 'the measure of the full stature of Christ'. It does not require suspending my judgment that some theological views are wrong, or that some views that are wrong may be actively harmful. It does require that I do not take it upon myself to limit that perceived harm by seeking to restrict the participation of those who hold such views in the common life of our church.

What does it mean for different (and even opposing) views to stand 'within the spectrum of teaching and tradition of the Anglican Communion'? Resolution III.2 of the 1998 Lambeth Conference called on the provinces of the Communion 'to affirm that those who dissent from, as well as those who assent to, the ordination of women to the priesthood and episcopate are both loyal Anglicans'. It is accordingly possible to hold the view that women can be bishops or the view that women cannot (or should not) be bishops and still be a faithful Anglican. In 20 out of the Anglican Communion's 39 Provinces, there is currently no legal impediment for the ordination of women to the three Orders. At the time of writing, 10 had actually ordained women as bishops. This situation is also relevant for the 'broader process of discernment' mentioned in the third Guiding Principle.

The House of Bishops' Declaration insists that: 'we have a duty to ensure that the welfare of the whole Church of England is sustained in all its theological depth and breadth'. Underpinning this is a commitment to unity-in-diversity within the church.[39] The desire to embrace diversity, within certain theological limits, springs in part from a view of the church as members of a family brought together as 'brothers and sisters in Christ, by the grace of God, with whom it is not possible to part.' As Archbishop Justin Welby declared in General Synod: 'You don't chuck out family, or even make it difficult for them to be at home; you love them and seek their well-being, even when you disagree'.[40]

Guiding Principle No. 5

- **Pastoral and sacramental provision for the minority within the Church of England will be made without specifying a limit of time and in a way that maintains the highest possible degree of communion and contributes to mutual flourishing across the whole Church of England.**

In order for those unable to receive the ministry of female bishops or priests to flourish in the 'life and structures' of the Church of England, specific pastoral and sacramental provision will need to be made, according to the fifth Guiding Principle, and it is to be made 'without specifying a limit of time'. The House of Bishops Declaration hopes that the arrangements will 'prove durable'.[41] Of course, those who believe that the decision to ordain women as well as men to all orders of ministry is right and brings blessing for Christ's church will hope and pray for the day when the whole Church of England and the whole Church of God can be united in the same judgment. Indeed, one of the characteristics of how the church lives with disagreement is that it refuses to give up on hoping for agreement that will enable us to be more fully one in our worship and our witness.[42] Yet this fifth Guiding Principle commits the Church of England to a certain restraint, as was noted above. Crucially, it will not seek to bring about greater agreement by penalising or restricting those who do not share the majority view on this matter. There needs to be confidence that a secure future within the Church of England remains for those whose theological convictions may mean they dissent from that view.[43]

The provisions are to be made in a way that 'maintains the highest possible degree of communion'. The concept of 'degrees' of communion originated in ecumenical ecclesiology, to affirm the communion between divided churches without denying the serious effects of that division.[44] At the 1988 and 1998 Lambeth Conferences, after some provinces began to ordain women, the idea was applied (already with some degree of paradox) to relations within the Anglican Communion itself.[45] It was sometimes linked to the language of 'impaired communion'.

This raises some sharp questions. How can the language of degrees of communion *between* churches be used to characterise relations *within* a church? In ecumenical ecclesiology, what constituted a body of Christians as a church was precisely being in communion with one another without qualification. Such communion included the common recognition of all ordained ministers, full sacramental sharing and the unity of the episcopate, as expressed for instance in participation in ordinations. Some have asked whether an ecclesial body can truly remain one church when deep fractures begin to affect these integral elements of communion.[46]

Three related responses might be offered to such questioning. First, it was already recognised in 1993 in *Bonds of Peace and Being in Communion* that ordaining women to the priesthood while making provision for those who did not accept their ministry as priests would change the way that the Church of England lived the communion that is Christ's gift. It was stated that:

The Church of England needs to understand itself as a communion in dialogue, committed to remaining together in the ongoing process of the discernment of truth within the wider fellowship of the Christian Church. Giving space to each other and remaining in the highest possible degree of communion in spite of difference are crucial, as we strive to be open to the insights of the wider Christian community. Though some of the means by which communion is expressed may be strained or broken, the need for courtesy, tolerance, mutual respect, prayer for one another and a continuing desire to know one another and to be with one another, remain binding upon us as Christians, no less within our own Church than is already the case in our ecumenical relations. The danger to be avoided is that, where ecclesial communion is impaired, communities may begin to define themselves over against one another and develop in isolation from each other.[47]

This passage implies a confidence that while profound disagreement can certainly destroy communion, it need not, if it can be held by those who continue to share in common things that profoundly unite them, centring for the church in participation in Christ and the sharing of his gospel.

Second, communion in the life of the church should not be limited only to the role of ordained ministers and the sacrament of the eucharist. It includes our common faith and doctrine, revealed in the Scriptures we read together; our 'structures of conciliar relations and decision-making', such as our synods; and our 'common witness and service in the world' – for the church is as truly the church in its being sent out to every nation as it is in the gathering together of the faithful.[48] Anglicans have also placed a particular emphasis on the importance of shared forms of public worship in sustaining our common life in the body of Christ.

These elements of ecclesial communion, as has already been emphasized, are not in question because of the decision to ordain women to the episcopate. Different theological convictions on the ordination of women remain 'within the spectrum of teaching and tradition of the Anglican Communion', since they do not detract from our common faith and common doctrine. All members of the Church of England remain governed by the same conciliar structures, all are subject to the same ecclesiastical law and none can step aside from the jurisdiction of the Ordinary because of their views on this matter. Despite those different views, parishes, priests and people engage in 'common witness and service in the world', for the sake of the gospel.

Third, the vulnerability of ecclesial communion is recognized in a new way, as something that cannot be taken for granted as simply there because we have certain institutional arrangements. With that comes a new consciousness of responsibility to aim for 'the highest possible degree of communion'. It would be easy to settle for much less and to accept the wisdom of the worldly maxim that good fences make good neighbours – that the simplest way to endure this impasse of disagreement is to ensure we have no more to do with one another than is strictly necessary, and the lines of separation are well-established. This fifth Guiding Principle is designed to provide a better way forward, in which we strive to outdo one another in love, preferring one another's interests to our own (Philippians 2.4).

The phrase 'mutual flourishing' needs to be understood in this context. It should not be taken to legitimate deepening separation, as though we will flourish more if we have less to do with one another. Flourishing means that we fulfil God's purpose for us, and the purpose of the church is communion with one another in the Lord Jesus Christ through the indwelling of the Holy Spirit. Nothing that diminishes that communion can promote our flourishing, but we also need to show respect and restraint in seeking one another's flourishing in the context of the necessary limitations that follow from our commitment to being a 'communion in dialogue' where there is no foreseeable prospect of coming to a common mind. The challenge is to accept those limitations and the lines of separation that follow from them, and then to take responsibility for the well-being within the body of Christ of those who are at times on the other side of those lines, and to rejoice when they are blessed with the gifts of the one Spirit.

The concept of mutuality is a well-developed theme, in the New Testament in particular.[49] Mutuality suggests partners of equal status and respect. The flourishing first mentioned in the fourth Guiding Principle must include a sense of relationship, or relationality, between parties who disagree, with the aim of building and showing trust, if it is to be genuinely mutual.

It also requires commitment and action from all. Yes, it relates to the provision of appropriate sacramental and pastoral ministry for those unable to accept women as bishops, as well as to their full and equal participation in all roles and institutional structures of the Church. Mutual flourishing must also refer to the flourishing of female clergy and bishops, and those who support them. That is not to say, however, that all this is only – or even mainly – about the clergy; the commitment given here is to 'mutual flourishing across the whole Church of England'. The whole Church of England encompasses the whole people of God, in a church characterized by resistance to any sharp demarcation between those who belong and those who do not. It includes those who have never heard of the Five Guiding Principles and have little if any idea of the issues that lie behind them, but want to attend a carol service in their neighbourhood at Christmas, get married in a church building they remember from childhood or for reasons they would struggle to explain bring their children for baptism.

The Five Guiding Principles hinge on an acceptance that our flourishing within the life of the church is bound up with the flourishing of others, including those with whom we disagree and with whom our communion within the church is consequently limited. Such a commitment to mutual flourishing does not come without serious costs, and it needs to be acknowledged that in different situations they may be unevenly distributed and fall more heavily on some for reasons not of their own choosing. All of this is a wound in the body, the pain of which we should not underestimate, and all our dealings under the Five Guiding Principles must be conducted in the light of this recognition.

That said, mutual flourishing cannot be a zero-sum game in which the flourishing of some can be imagined as coming only at the cost of the diminishment of others. Yes, the presence of ordained women inevitably limits the participation in the life of the church of those who do not accept their ministry, while that absence of acceptance in turn restricts the fullness of the ministry of ordained women in various ways, some of them far-reaching. Without denying those realities, to seek mutual flourishing is to focus on what it means for all to enter more deeply together into the kingdom of the beloved Son, trusting that for those who seek first the kingdom of God, the things we worry about losing will turn out by God's grace to be added to us as well.

Chapter 3: **Living it Out**

Disagreement is a normal part of the life of the church on earth. The church's participation through history in the mission of God is always opening new horizons, and with them new questions that cannot always be easily or quickly settled. What should make the church distinctive as human community and institution is not immunity from disagreement, but the situating of disagreement within our life together as the body of Christ, as those who have heard the good news of Christ and who long to share it with others.[50] The challenge of living out the Five Guiding Principles needs to be set within this wider context of what it means to disagree with one another as those who are bound together in communion within the church.

The early Church grew amidst negotiations, contestations and arguments. It faced disagreements over the divinity of Jesus Christ (the Arian controversy), over questions of complicity with political power (the Donatist controversy), over the question of sin in relation to nature and grace (the Pelagian controversy), and countless others. Church councils provided a vital context for debate and deliberation, but force was also applied in various ways in the cause of finding a way forward. Sometimes the settlements that emerged had a dimension of compromise, and aimed to enable opposing parties to carry on worshiping together; sometimes, as in the case of the Donatists, they did not, and the majority sought to compel the minority to conform to its ways.

The doctrinal statements we inherit from this formative period are marked by both clarity and openness. The Church came to affirm God as triune (three persons in one being); it affirmed Jesus Christ as fully divine and fully human (two natures in one hypostasis). There is enough clarity to end one kind of argument. But there is also enough openness to allow an on-going process of theological exploration and interpretation that generates arguments of its own. It is a vital principle of good theology that one only seeks the clarity one needs, for the time being, in order to go on together.

The Church of England has its own particular history of living with disagreement. In the midst of the controversies triggered by the Protestant Reformation of the 16th century, it sought to define parameters for doctrine and practice – including, crucially, worship – within which those holding a range of views on disputed questions of the day could live together as one church in and for one nation. Its historic formularies include the Articles of Religion, along with the Book of Common Prayer and the Ordinal as received from the sixteenth and seventeenth centuries, but not anything like a set of magisterial documents to set alongside those of Roman Catholicism.

It would be easy to fall into a romantic view of this legacy, forgetful of the levels of coercion and violence involved until at least the 19th century in achieving the social and political uniformity which enabled the Church of England to consider itself the one church of the nation. It is however a history that makes clear that the Church of England has at various points resisted seeking the decisive resolution of doctrinal arguments, but has relied on being able to reach an at times uneasy peace between differing groups of Christians who continue to belong within one body. Anglican theology is beautifully clear on some central issues, but is polyphonic and pragmatic on others. Our life together in communion has never been guaranteed by the clarity of Anglican doctrine on every matter of controversy, but by institutional habits that enable us to live with each other's disappointing failures and objectionable views, within certain limits. The church is not primarily a polyphony of positions, however, but a communion of persons. It is not first and foremost a pragmatism of settlements but a family of worshippers who seek to worship God together in Spirit and in truth. There are rules to live by, but these are there to protect and promote the flourishing of its members, who share their life with one another as a communion of persons in the one Lord Jesus Christ.

The reference to 'the minority' in the fifth Guiding Principle is worth reflecting on in this context. Who is in the minority regarding acceptance of female clergy rather depends on whom we are counting in the first place, but in terms of the Church of England, it is clear enough that there is a majority and a minority position. It may be tempting for the majority to think that, were the minority to leave or disappear, the 'problem' posed by their existence would be resolved and all the energy unfortunately required to manage it be liberated for more productive endeavours. It may be tempting for the minority to think that the more they can separate themselves from the majority and insulate themselves from its influence, the more secure their survival will be. These two tendencies are, of course, mutually reinforcing. To succumb to them is, however, not only to go directly against the grain of the Five Guiding Principles. It is to give up on the idea that part of the distinctive witness of Anglicanism to society and to the wider church is how it enables those who hold views at variance with the majority in some matters to flourish within a family of worshippers who seek to serve God together, sustaining a communion of persons whose serious, painful and hard-to-manage disagreements do not corrode their commitment to love one another as Christ has loved them.

It is important to situate the Five Guiding Principles within such historical and doctrinal perspectives. Yet while their adoption by the Church of England can be seen as part of the developing and to some extent distinctive tradition of Anglicanism more generally within global Christianity, what are some of the specific issues emerging for those who are currently living them out? How are they shaping the life of the Church of England here and now, and what kind of questions might they be raising for the future?

The Five Guiding Principles form part of a Declaration from the House of Bishops, one of whose key concerns was to set out a clear process for parishes that cannot receive the ministry of women priests and bishops because of theological conviction to receive a suitable form of extended episcopal oversight. Since 2015, there has been a steady stream of parishes seeking to make use of this provision, while some parishes that had made use of it have decided it is no longer required. In general, this appear to happen without undue stresses on relations between the parish and the diocese; the lack of use to date of the grievance procedure that was established for PCCs in 2014 might be noted in this regard.[51] The effective working of the practical arrangements has helped to give confidence that the Five Guiding Principles can find expression in how the question of 'pastoral and sacramental provision' is dealt with on the ground.

This is not to say, of course, that all is simple and straightforward. The challenges of living out the Principles were underlined repeatedly in key speeches from 2014, as the Introduction to this text noted, and they have by no means gone away. Yet there is also plenty of evidence of the willingness to meet those challenges, and of scope for creative imagination in reaching across profound differences to seek one another's flourishing in the 'highest possible degree of communion'. An example of this is given on the next page.

Within the Diocese of Exeter there are those who have found my appointment as a woman bishop difficult. In meeting with them I have developed trusted relationships and an understanding of how we can offer ministry together. This has always started with a conversation about how I can enable their ministry to flourish and how will we relate in a way which respects our theological difference.

The Bishop of Ebbsfleet and I have established a good working relationship. We have sat together on interview panels for priests in parishes under his oversight and we have shared responsibility for pastoral issues related to clergy in Devon who look to his oversight. I have been able to preach in a number of churches in which Bishop Jonathan has been invited to exercise pastoral and sacramental ministry, and working together we are looking to opportunities to model the Five Guiding Principles in undertaking shared study days and retreats and in shared worship.

I have ensured that the Five Guiding Principles are explored not only with those who don't accept my ministry, but also with those who do, and I will be sharing a session on our local ministerial training scheme in the new year with two colleagues, one from Forward in Faith and one from Reform, to talk about how we undertake ministry together.

The Rt Reverend Sarah Mullally
Bishop of Crediton
November 2017

Some brief consideration might also be given to the work of the Independent Reviewer, the creation of whose role was an integral component of the 2014 House of Bishops' Declaration. To date, reports have been published by the Independent Reviewer on three 'concerns' referred to him under the regulations for resolution of disputes agreed by the House of Bishops in 2014. These are: the celebration of separate Chrism Masses by clergy who do not accept the ordination of women to the priesthood and episcopate; the licensing of female priests to multi-parish benefices where one parish had indicated its wish 'to take advantage of arrangements available to those whose theological conviction leads them to seek the priestly or episcopal ministry of men' under the House of Bishops' Declaration in 2014 (phrase from paragraph 20); and Bishop Philip North's appointment to and subsequent withdrawal from the See of Sheffield.

These cases highlight in different ways the potential tension between the three carefully coordinated elements of the fifth Principle: making 'pastoral and sacramental provision for the minority'; maintaining 'the highest possible degree of communion'; and seeking 'mutual flourishing'. Does holding separate Chrism Masses within a single diocese, for instance, represent appropriate 'pastoral and sacramental provision for the minority', or does it institutionalise something substantially less than 'the highest possible degree of communion' that could and should be maintained as priests renew their ordination vows, receive oils for their ministry that have been blessed by their bishop and prepare for the Solemn Triduum?

The Independent Reviewer concluded that such provision in this case was not contrary to the Five Guiding Principles. There is perhaps a recurring issue here, however, about what it means within a single church to hold distinct sacramental and collegial spaces, in which not all who participate in one can participate in the other in the same way. The establishment, for instance, of The Society under the patronage of Saint Wilfrid and Saint Hilda has done much to give confidence regarding their continuing place within the Church of England to those whose reservations about female clergy derive from concern for catholic order. Something similar might be said about the appointment of the Revd Rod Thomas as a Provincial Episcopal Visitor in 2015 with regard to those whose reservations derive from concern for obedience to scripture. The 'ecology' of the Church of England has developed in some significant ways since 2014, and it will doubtless continue to do so. When does 'mutual flourishing' mean making space for those with different theological convictions to do the things of the church apart from one another, when does it call us to do those things together, and when does it require a willingness to move between the different sacramental and collegial spaces thus created?

If love for one another may sometimes mean allowing the creation of distinct spaces, with certain lines drawn around them, it must also mean a willingness to keep crossing these boundaries where it is possible to do so and thus prevent them turning into entrenched barriers. Such boundary-crossing becomes crucial as a way of maintaining 'the highest possible degree of communion'. It is also essential if we are to seek the flourishing in Christ of those on the other side of the boundary that we know them first and foremost as fellow members of the body of Christ, in worship, witness and discipleship. Finally, that some people move between the different sacramental and collegial spaces that now exist within the church is also vital for preventing the associated boundaries from accruing undue weight, such that those on each side start to think and behave as a separate church, which has no need for or interest in the others.

The need for that movement between different spaces within the life of the one Church of England has an important corollary. All have an obligation to foster the kind of hospitality that enables this movement to happen. Such hospitality is not about the denial of differences or of continuing disagreements, but it does mean, for instance, accepting invitations to meet with one another where circumstances do not prevent it. It means a willingness to respond to communication in a way that will build up relationships in the body of Christ and strengthen one another in faith. It means making those who would not normally attend 'our' service or gathering welcome, and including them in as much of what is happening as is possible. It means heeding Paul's command to the Christians of Rome in the face of their own serious disagreements: 'Welcome one another, therefore, just as Christ has welcomed you, for the glory of God' (Romans 15.7).

The Five Guiding Principles cannot be used mechanically to determine the answers to every question that arises from the Church of England's decision in 2014 to ordain women to the episcopate. What they provide is a way to frame those questions that all can share and that can thereby help us to talk to and with, and not past or at, one another. As was stated in a previous Faith and Order Commission report, 'judgments about what to do always depend on descriptions of the situation we are facing, and such descriptions are always informed by theological and philosophical commitments, however unarticulated and unacknowledged they may be.'[52] Part of the purpose of the Five Guiding Principles is to provide a description of the situation the Church of England is in following the decision to open all three orders of ministry to men and women equally: a description consciously informed by theological commitments that can then shape the way that judgments about what to do in various circumstances are made.

In every concrete situation, there will be a number of courses of action that could be taken; the Five Guiding Principles will rarely if ever point to just one of them. The description they give, informed by theological commitments, will shape, not determine, the work of forming a judgment. It would be quite wrong, therefore, to use them as way of closing down conversation and debate about the view that is to be taken in a particular situation. They will in some cases identify certain courses of action as out of bounds, and others as fitting with – which does not mean required by – the path that the Church of England has chosen to walk. They cannot therefore substitute for the hard work of deliberation, discernment and judgment that is continually required in the life of the church – and the Church of England has consistently shown a strong concern to attend to the particularity of each pastoral situation. Such judgment must always be illuminated by love – love that has regard to the relative distributions of power and status with a particular care for those who have least. Only in the light of God's love for us, and of the love for one another that is both Christ's command and his gift, will we be able to see and do what God asks of us.

Chapter 4   Some Questions for Further Reflection

A number of significant theological issues have been identified in the course of this brief document, whose analysis at various point draws on the earlier report of the Faith and Order Commission, *Communion and Disagreement*. This short final chapter identifies four key theological concepts or pairs of concepts to have emerged from that analysis: respect and recognition; discernment and reception; flourishing; and communion. It quotes a brief passage from the section of the document that is particularly relevant for each of these and suggests some questions for further reflection, before turning to the challenge of reading the Five Guiding Principles together.

The questions may be a useful starting point for groups who want to engage in dialogue together about what it means to be guided by the Five Guiding Principles in their specific context within the Church of England.

Respect and recognition (first and second Guiding Principles):

> *... careful consideration of what we do 'recognize' in one another, and of the best theological description that can be offered for that, is needed if 'respect' is to be fully expressed and communicated as a characteristic of our relationships.'*
>
> *(page 21)*

- What can female clergy in the Church of England hope for by way of 'respect' from those who because of theological conviction do not accept certain aspects of their ministry?

- What kind of 'recognition' might those who do not accept certain aspects of their ministry be able to give them? How different might the issues be in this regard for Evangelicals and Anglo-Catholics?

- What kind of 'recognition' and 'respect' can those who do not support the ordination of women as priests and bishops expect from those who support it, especially where the latter are in a position of oversight and authority? Does it make a difference if the people in that position are female clergy?

Discernment and reception (third Guiding Principle):

The focus in the third Guiding Principle, however, is specifically on discernment as a task that cannot be undertaken by the Church of England in isolation, but which it addresses as a church within the Anglican Communion and as a part of the whole Church of God. Its having come to 'a clear decision on the matter' does not mean that it has no interest or part in the 'wider process of discernment' that is continuing.

(page 27)

- What might the Church of England contribute to 'the process of discernment within the Anglican Communion and the whole Church of God' on this matter?

- What might the Church of England expect to receive from that process?

- How should the Church of England's teaching that it is part of the one, holy, catholic and apostolic church be expressed in the way it deliberates and makes decisions about issues like this?

Flourishing (fourth and fifth Guiding Principles):

To 'flourish' has connotations of to prosper, to thrive, to grow – not to shrink out and die. It means prayerfully encouraging all within the Church of England, that they might prove fruitful in proclaiming the kingdom of God, not wanting any to dwindle or fail. It means not corralling some within the boundaries of their own parishes or networks, but providing space generously for all to flourish in its common life and in structures shared by all.

(page 29)

- Where might we look in Scripture for teaching about what flourishing means for those who follow the way of Christ?

- If the Five Guiding Principles commit us to seeking the flourishing of people who hold different views from our own, do they also commit us to seeking the flourishing of the groups and institutions that promote those views?

The Five Guiding Principles

- How adequate do you find the account provided in this text of how we might seek the flourishing within the church of those whose views we find harmful and to that extent detrimental to the flourishing of the church (pages 29-30)? Could a better account be given?

Communion (fifth Guiding Principle):

How can the language of degrees of communion between churches be used to characterise relations within a church? In ecumenical ecclesiology, what constituted a body of Christians as a church was precisely being in communion with one another without qualification. Such communion included the common recognition of all ordained ministers, full sacramental sharing and the unity of the episcopate, as expressed for instance in participation in ordinations.

(page 33)

- Does commitment to the Five Guiding Principles fatally undermine the communion supposed to unite the church, or does it make sense to say (as argued above, and in the Faith and Order Commission report on Communion and Disagreement) that such disagreement impairs but does not break our communion as one church?

- Is there a tension between maintaining the highest possible degree of communion and seeking mutual flourishing (because mutual flourishing requires a degree of separation), or are they properly convergent (because communion is integral to our flourishing, as is argued on page 36)?

- What opportunities might you have for the 'boundary-crossing' and 'hospitality' that the document argues are key to maintaining the highest possible degree of communion in the present context (pages 46–7)?

The Five Guiding Principles need to be 'read one with the other and held together in tension':

- After reading this document, what would you identify as the key points of tension that arise from holding the Five Guiding Principles together?

- Are there particular Guiding Principles or phrases within them that you find difficult to understand, struggle to accept or simply think are wrong?

- Do some of the Guiding Principles build on others, do they form a sequence, or are they all equally foundational and capable of being read in any order?

- If you could do so, is there a Sixth Guiding Principle you would now like to add?

Notes

1. GS Misc 1076 [*House of Bishops' Declaration on the Ministry of Bishops and Priests*], Paragraph 5, pp. 1–2. URL: http://www.ministrydevelopment.org.uk/UserFiles/File/ TRIG/gs_misc_1076_women_in_the_episcopate_house_of_bishops_declaration.pdf.
2. HL Paper 45, HC 622 [*House of Lords and House of Commons Ecclesiastical Committee. Bishops and Priests (Consecration and Ordination of Women) Measure, 233rd Report*], p. 9 of the attached Tuesday 22 July 2014 Deliberation with the Assistance of Representatives of the General Synod. URL: https://publications. parliament.uk/pa/jt201415/jtselect/jtecc/45/45.pdf.
3. *Report of Proceedings 2014, General Synod, February Group of Sessions*, vol. 45, no. 1, p. 158. URL: https://www.churchofengland.org/sites/default/files/2017-10/Final% 20Version%20of%20RoP%20with%20Index%20%28Feb%20%202014%29.pdf.
4. See also the comments of the Archbishop of Canterbury on Newsnight [14 July 2014], 'the biggest change of the last 20 months has been the way we treat each other and the way we are learning to treat people we disagree with.' URL: https://www.youtube. com/watch?v=ZhyknRwbNW4.
5. Miroslav Volf defines 'flourishing' as 'the life that is lived well, the life that goes well, and the life that feels good – all three together, inextricably intertwined' (*Flourishing: Why We Need Religion in a Globalized World* (New Haven: Yale University Press, 2016), p. ix).
6. *Official Report, House of Lords*, 4 October 2014; vol. 756, c. 187. URL: http://hansard. parliament.uk/lords/2014-10-14/debates/14101484000208/Bishops AndPriests (ConsecrationAndOrdinationOfWomen)Measure#187. See also the comment in GS Misc 1077 [*House of Bishops' Declaration on the Ministry of Bishops and Priests: Guidance Note from the House*] that the principles are 'designed to sustain the diversity of the Church of England and the mutual flourishing of its constituent parts' (p. 2). URL: https://www.churchofengland.org/sites/default/files/2017-11/GS%20Misc%201077 %20House%20of%20Bishops%20Declaration%20on%20the%20Ministry%20 of%20Bishops%20and%20Priests%20%20Guidance%20note%20from%20the%20 House.pdf.
7. *Report of Proceedings 2014, General Synod, July Group Sessions*, vol. 45, no. 2, p. 311. URL: https://www.churchofengland.org/sites/default/files/2017-10/ Report%20of%20Proceedings%20with%20Index%20%28July%202014%29.pdf.
8. See Martin Warner, 'In Love and Charity with your Neighbour' in *Fathers in God*, ed. Colin Podmore (Norwich: Canterbury Press, 2015), pp. 3ff.
9. Women began to be ordained as deacons in the Church of England in 1987.
10. See Chapter 4, 'The development of women's ministry in the Church of England' in *Women Bishops in the Church of England?: A Report of the House of Bishops' Working*

Party on Women in the Episcopate (London: Church House Publishing, 2004), p. 119; Colin Podmore, 'Synodical Government in the Church of England, illustrated by the case of the ordination of women to the priesthood,' in *Aspects of Anglican Identity* (London: Church House Publishing, 2005), pp. 124–33.

11 On the role of the Ecclesiastical Committee in this matter, see Judith Maltby, 'Gender and Establishment: Parliament, "Erastianism" and the Ordination of Women 1993–2010,' in Mark Chapman, Judith Maltby and William Whyte (eds.), *The Established Church: Past, Present and Future* (London: T&T Clark, 2011), pp. 98–123.

12 Fuller references: attachment to GS 1074, 'Bonds of Peace: Arrangements for the Pastoral Care following the Ordination of Women to the Priesthood in the Church of England', and GS Misc 418 [*Being in Communion*].

13 *Women Bishops in the Church of England: A Report of the House of Bishops Working Party on Women in the Episcopate* (London: Church House Publishing, 2004).

14 GS 1886 [*Women in the Episcopate – New Legislative Proposals: Report from the House of Bishops*]. URL: https://www.canterburydiocese.org/media/synods/diocesan/june2013/gs%201886%20-%20women%20in%20the%20episcopate%20-%20new%20legislative%20proposals.pdf.

15 GS Misc 1076. URL: http://www.ministrydevelopment.org.uk/UserFiles/File/TRIG/gs_misc_1076_women_in_the_episcopate_house_of_bishops_declaration.pdf.

16 At its meeting in September 2014, the Ministry Council approved a proposal to require all candidates coming to BAPs and at the end of their training to indicate their assent to the Five Guiding Principles.

17 Rupert Bursell, 'The Oath of Canonical Obedience', *Ecclesiastical Law Journal* 16 (May 2014): pp. 168–186.

18 Cf. GS Misc 1076 [*House of Bishops' Declaration on the Ministry of Bishops and Priests*], paragraph 36, p. 7. URL: http://www.ministrydevelopment.org.uk/UserFiles/File/TRIG/gs_misc_1076_women_in_the_episcopate_house_of_bishops_declaration. pdf.

19 HL Paper 45, HC 622 [*House of Lords and House of Commons Ecclesiastical Committee. Bishops and Priests (Consecration and Ordination of Women) Measure, 233rd Report*], p. 9 of the attached Tuesday 22 July 2014 Deliberation with the Assistance of Representatives of the General Synod.

20 'Ordinary' here means having the spiritual jurisdiction of the diocese by virtue of holding the office of diocesan bishop.

21 Transcript of speech on http://rowanwilliams.archbishopofcanterbury.org/articles.php/2349/general-synod-archbishop-rowan-speaks-in-debate-on-women-bishops#Transcript.

22 Cf. GS Misc 1139 [*Communion and Disagreement: A Report from the Faith and Order Commission*] paragraphs 67–68, pp. 31–32.

URL: https://www.churchofengland.org/sites/default/files/201710/communion_and_ disagreement_faoc_report_gs_misc_1139.pdf.

23 GS 1951 [*Draft Bishops and Priests (Consecration and Ordination of Women) Measure and Draft Amending Canon No. 33: Report by the Business Committee on the Reference to the Dioceses*] Annex A.

24 *Report of Proceedings 2014: General Synod, July Group of Proceedings*, vol. 45, no. 2, p. 315. URL: https://www.churchofengland.org/sites/default/files/2017-10/ Report%20of%20Proceedings%20with%20Index%20%28July%202014%29.pdf.

25 The Lambeth Appeal to All Christian People in 1920 argued that the episcopate was the 'one means' of providing 'a ministry acknowledged by every part of the Church as possessing not only the inward call of the Spirit, but also the commission of Christ and the authority of the whole body.' Cf. Lambeth Conference 1920, Resolution 9.VI-VII, and URL: http://www.anglicancommunion.org/media/127731/1920.pdf.

26 The Lambeth Conference, Resolutions Archive from 1988, p. 4. URL: http://www. anglicancommunion.org/media/127749/1988.pdf.

27 For texts of the resolutions, see URL: http://www.anglicancommunion.org/media/ 76650/1998.pdf.

28 Attachment to GS 1074: 'Bonds of Peace': 'Arrangements for the Pastoral Care following the Ordination of Women to the Priesthood in the Church of England', paragraph 3, p. 6.

29 Ibid., paragraph 3, p. 5.

30 Cardinal Walter Kasper, 'Mission of Bishops in the Mystery of the Church: Reflections on the question of ordaining women to episcopal office in the Church of England.' URL: http://www.vatican.va/roman_curia/pontifical_councils/chrstuni/card-kasper-docs/rc_pc_chrstuni_doc_20060605_kasper-bishops_en.html.

31 Cf. GS Misc 1139 [*Communion and Disagreement: A Report from the Faith and Order Commission*] Paragraph 72, p. 39. URL: https://www.churchofengland.org/sites/default/ files/2017-10/communion_and_disagreement_faoc_report_gs_misc_1139.pdf.

32 First Anglican Roman Catholic International Commission, Authority in the Church I (1976), I.2. URL: http://www.vatican.va/roman_curia/pontifical_councils/chrstuni/ angl-comm-docs/rc_pc_chrstuni_doc_197609_authority-church-i_en.html.

33 It also appears, for instance, in the Cyprus Statement 2006 [*The Church of the Triune God, The Cyprus Statement agreed by the International Commission for Anglican-Orthodox Theological Dialogue 2006*] to denote 'part of the ongoing life of the Church', by which the gospel and the things of the Spirit are received by the church (cf. pp. 97-98). URL: http://www.anglicancommunion.org/media/103818/The-Church-of-the-Triune-God.pdf. For its relevance to debates on the ordination of women, see e.g. Paul Avis (ed.), *Seeking the Truth of Change in the Church: Reception, Communion and the*

Ordination of Women (London: T&T Clark, 2004), and more recently Avis, 'Bishops in Communion? The Unity of the Episcopate, the Unity of the Diocese and the Unity of the Church', *Ecclesiology* 13 (2017): 299–323.

34 Introducing the Report of the Steering Committee for the Draft Legislation on Women in the Episcopate (GS 1924), November 2013.

35 See GS Misc 1076 [*Women in the Episcopate: House of Bishops' Declaration on the Ministry of Bishops and Priests*] paragraphs 9 & 10. URL: http://www.ministry development.org.uk/UserFiles/File/TRIG/gs_misc_1076_women_in_the_episcopate_ house_of_bishops_declaration.pdf.

36 *Priests (Ordination of Women) Measure 1993, Code of Practice, Issued by the authority of the House of Bishops, January 1994* [London: General Synod of the Church of England] Appendix A (Episcopal Ministry Act of Synod 1993), page 1.

37 Cf. footnote 27, p. 55 of *Review of Nomination to the See of Sheffield and Related Concerns: Report by the Independent Reviewer* [Sir Philip Mawer], September 2017. URL: https://www.churchofengland.org/sites/default/files/2017-11/Review%20of% 20the%20Nomination%20to%20the%20See%20of%20Sheffield%20and%20 Related%20Concerns%20Appendices.pdf.

38 GS Misc 1076 [*Women in the Episcopate: House of Bishops' Declaration on the Ministry of Bishops and Priests*] Statement 15, p. 3. URL: http://www.ministry development.org.uk/UserFiles/File/TRIG/gs_misc_1076_women_in_the_episcopate_ house_of_bishops_declaration.pdf.

39 Jonathan Goodall and Jeremy Worthen, 'The Limits of Diversity', in *Supporting Papers for the Faith and Order Commission Report, Communion and Disagreement,* pp. 62–72. URL: https://www.churchofengland.org/sites/default/files/2017-10/ communion_and_ disagreement_supporting_papers.pdf.

40 *Report of Proceedings 2014, General Synod, July Group of Sessions,* vol. 45, no. 2, p. 311.

41 GS Misc 1076 [*Women in the Episcopate: House of Bishops' Declaration on the Ministry of Bishops and Priests*], paragraph 39, p. 8. URL: http://www.ministry development.org.uk/UserFiles/File/TRIG/gs_misc_1076_women_in_the_episcopate_ house_of_bishops_declaration.pdf.

42 This was a key theme in GS Misc 1139 [*Communion and Disagreement: A Report from the Faith and Order Commission*]. See e.g. Paragraphs 13, 17, 25 and especially 73ff. URL: https://www.churchofengland.org/sites/default/files/2017-10/ communion_and_disagreement_faoc_report_gs_misc_1139.pdf.

43 Several speakers in the July 2014 final approval debate spoke about the need for the durability of the provisions: 'I hope that the promised commitment of mutual

flourishing is not a commitment that will run out of steam in a few years but is a commitment that will continue for 50 and 100 years' (Adrian Vincent). See Report of Proceedings 2014: General Synod July Group of Sessions, vol. 45, no. 2., p. 286. URL: https://www.churchofengland.org/sites/default/files/2017-10/Report%20of% 20Proceedings%20with%20Index%20%28July%202014%29.pdf.

44 Cf. the Second Vatican Council's Decree on Ecumenism, *Unitatis redintegratio*, chapter I.3 (URL: http://www.vatican.va/archive/hist_councils/ii_vatican_council/documents/ vat-ii_decree_19641121_unitatis-redintegratio_en.html), and GS Misc 1139 *[Communion and Disagreement: A Report from the Faith and Order Commission]*, pp. 25ff, Paragraphs 46–50, 66–67, 77. URL: https://www.churchofengland.org/sites/ default/files/2017-10/communion_and_disagreement_faoc_report_gs_misc_1139.pdf.

45 Resolution I.1 of the 1988 Lambeth Conference affirms 'that each Province respect the decision and attitudes of other provinces in the ordination or consecration of women to the episcopate, without such respect necessarily indicating acceptance of the principles involved, maintaining the highest possible degree of communion with the provinces which differ.' URL: http://www.anglicancommunion.org/media/ 127749/1988.pdf. Resolution III.2 of the 1998 Lambeth Conference also affirmed that 'although some of the means by which communion is expressed may be strained or broken, there is a need for courtesy, tolerance, mutual respect, and prayer for one another, and we confirm that our desire to know or be with one another, remains binding on us as Christians' (Eames, p.119). URL: http://www.anglicancommunion. org/media/76650/1998.pdf.

46 Paul Avis, 'Bishops in Communion? The Unity of the Episcopate, the Unity of the Diocese and the Unity of the Church' *Ecclesiology* 13 (2017): 299–323.

47 Attachment to GS 1074: 'Bonds of Peace': Arrangements for the Pastoral Care following the Ordination of Women to the Priesthood in the Church of England', paragraph 3, p. 6; quoted in *Review of Nomination to the See of Sheffield and Related Concerns: Report by the Independent Reviewer* [Sir Philip Mawer], September 2017, p. 55. URL: https://www.churchofengland.org/sites/default/files/2017-11/Review%20of%20the %20Nomination%20to%20the%20See%20of%20Sheffield%20and%20Related%20Co ncerns%20Appendices.pdf.

48 From World Council of Churches 'The Church: Local and Universal'(1990) §25, quoted in World Council of Churches Faith and Order Paper No. 214 [*The Church: Towards a Common Vision*], p. 22 (URL: https://www.oikoumene.org/en/resources/ documents/commissions/faith-and-order/i-unity-the-church-and-its-mission/the- church-towards-a-common-vision/@@download/file/The_Church_Towards_a_ common_vision.pdf) and Paragraph 43 of GS Misc 1139 [*Communion and*

Disagreement: A Report from the Faith and Order Commission], p. 22
(URL: https://www.churchofengland.org/sites/default/files/2017-10/communion_
and_disagreement_faoc_report_gs_misc_1139.pdf).
49 See e.g. Ephesians 5.21. Mutuality is one of the three accompanying themes to the
five Guiding Principles in the House of Bishops' Declaration, which states: 'Mutuality
reflects the Church of England's wider commitment to sustaining diversity. It means
that those of differing conviction will be committed to making it possible for each other
to flourish' (paragraph 14 of GS Misc 1076, URL: http://www.ministrydevelopment.
org.uk/UserFiles/File/TRIG/gs_misc_1076_women_in_the_episcopate_house_of_
bishops_declaration.pdf). Gordon McConville offers an examination of various kinds
of familial relating in the Old Testament, concluding that 'These have in common with
that other biblical construct of covenant their power to suggest that mutuality and
loyalty are indispensable to human flourishing' (*Being Human in God's World* (Grand
Rapids, Michigan: Baker Academic 2016), p. 169).
50 Cf. GS Misc 1139 [*Communion and Disagreement: A Report from the Faith and Order
Commission*] Paragraphs 1–11, 18. URL: https://www.churchofengland.org/sites/
default/files/2017-10/communion_and_disagreement_faoc_report_gs_misc_1139.pdf.
51 GS Misc 1087 [*Declaration on the Ministry of Bishops and Priests (Resolution of
Disputes Procedure) Regulations 2014: Regulations Made by the House of Bishops
under Canon C 29*]. URL: https://www.churchofengland.org/sites/default/files/
2017-11/GS%20Misc%201087%20-%20dispute%20resolution%20procedure%20
regulations%20under%20canon%20c.29.pdf.
52 GS Misc 1139 [*Communion and Disagreement: A Report from the Faith and Order
Commission*], paragraph 6, p. 6. URL: https://www.churchofengland.org/sites/
default/files/2017-10/communion_and_disagreement_faoc_report_gs_misc_1139.pdf.

Selected Further Reading

General Synod papers

GS 1074, *Bonds of Peace: Arrangements for the Pastoral Care following the Ordination of Women to the Priesthood in the Church of England*, June 1993

GS Misc 418, *Being in Communion*, June 1993

GS Misc 1076, *House of Bishops' Declaration on the Ministry of Bishops and Priests*, June 2014. URL: https://www.churchofengland.org/sites/default/files/2017-11/GS%20Misc%201076%20Women%20in%20the%20Episcopate.pdf

GS Misc 1077, *House of Bishops' Declaration on the Ministry of Bishops and Priests: Guidance Note from the House,* June 2014. URL: https://www.churchofengland.org/sites/default/files/2017-11/GS%20Misc%201077%20House%20of%20Bishops%20Declaration%20on%20the%20Ministry%20of%20Bishops%20and%20Priests%20-%20Guidance%20note%20from%20the%20House.pdf

GS Misc 1139, *Communion and Disagreement: A Report from the Faith and Order Commission*, June 2016. URL: https://www.churchofengland.org/sites/default/files/201710/communion_and_disagreement_faoc_report_gs_misc_1139.pdf

Other Church of England documents

Women Bishops in the Church of England?: A Report of the House of Bishops' Working Party on Women in the Episcopate (London: Church House Publishing, 2004)

Bishop of Sheffield's Ministry Provision Advisory Group, *New Norms New Beginnings*, March 2015. URL: http://www.sheffield.anglican.org/UserFiles/File/New_Norms_New_Beginning_FINAL_.pdf

Review of Nomination to the See of Sheffield and Related Concerns: Report by the Independent Reviewer [Sir Philip Mawer], September 2017. URL: https://www.churchofengland.org/sites/default/files/ 2017-11/Review%20of%20the%20Nomination%20to%20the%20 See%20of%20Sheffield%20and%20Related%20Concerns.pdf (main report); https://www.churchofengland.org/sites/default/ files/2017-11/Review%20of%20the%20Nomination%20to%20the% 20See%20of%20Sheffield%20and%20Related%20Concerns%20 Appendices.pdf (appendices)

Other material

Paul Avis, ed., *Seeking the Truth of Change in the Church: Reception, Communion and the Ordination of Women* (London: T&T Clark, 2004)

Paul Avis, 'Bishops in Communion? The Unity of the Episcopate, the Unity of the Diocese and the Unity of the Church,' *Ecclesiology* 13 (2017): 299–323

Rupert Bursell, 'The Oath of Canonical Obedience', *Ecclesiastical Law Journal* 16 (May 2014): 168–186

Lis Goddard and Clare Hendry 'From Castles to Conversations: Reflections on How to Disagree Well,' in Andrew Atherstone and Andrew Goddard, eds., *Good Disagreement?: Grace and Truth in a Divided Church* (Oxford: Lion, 2015), pp. 151–70

Jonathan Goodall and Jeremy Worthen, 'The Limits of Diversity,' in *Supporting Papers for the Faith and Order Commission Report*, Communion and Disagreement, 2016, pp. 62–74. URL: https:// www.churchofengland.org/sites/default/files/2017-10/communion_ and_disagreement_supporting_papers.pdf

Cardinal Walter Kasper, 'Mission of Bishops in the Mystery of the Church: Reflections on the Question of Ordaining Women to Episcopal Office in the Church of England,' 2006. URL: http://www.vatican.va/roman_curia/pontifical_councils/chrstuni/card-kasper-docs/rc_pc_chrstuni_doc_20060605_kasper-bishops_en.html

Judith Maltby, 'Gender and Establishment: Parliament, "Erastianism" and the Ordination of Women 1993–2010,' in Mark Chapman, Judith Maltby and William Whyte, eds., *The Established Church: Past, Present and Future* (London: T&T Clark, 2011), pp. 98–123

Martyn Percy, 'A Clash of Cultures: Church Autonomy and Human Rights,' in *Salt of the Earth: Religious Resilience in a Secular Age* (London: Sheffield Academic Press, 2002); reproduced in appendices to *Review of Nomination to the See of Sheffield and Related Concerns: Report by the Independent Reviewer* (details above)

Colin Podmore, ed., *Fathers in God: Resources for Reflection on Women in the Episcopate* (Norwich: Canterbury Press, 2015)

Colin Podmore, 'Synodical Government in the Church of England, Illustrated by the Case of the Ordination of Women to the Priesthood,' in *Aspects of Anglican Identity* (London: Church House Publishing, 2005), pp. 124–33

Society of St Wilfrid and St Hilda, *Catholicity and Communion in the Church of England: A Statement of Principles by the Council of Bishops of the Society*, 2015. URL: http://www.sswsh.com/uploads/Communion_and_Catholicity_for_web.pdf